KT-555-850

fife
C O U N C I L
KING'S ROAD PRIMARY SCHOOL
KING'S CRESCENT
ROSYTH
FIFE KY11 2RS

THEN & NOW

fARMING

Written by Katie Roden
Illustrated by James Field & Stephen Sweet

COPPER BEECH BOOKS
BROOKFIELD, CONNECTICUT

© Aladdin Books Ltd
1996

Designed and produced by
Aladdin Books Ltd
28 Percy Street
London W1P 0LD

First published in the United States in 1996 by
Copper Beech Books,
an imprint of
The Millbrook Press
2 Old New Milford Road
Brookfield
Connecticut 06804

Editor
Jon Richards
Design
David West Children's
Book Design
Designers
Flick Killerby
Edward Simkins
Picture Research
Brooks Krikler
Research
Illustrators
James Field, Stephen
Sweet – Simon Girling
& Associates

Printed in Belgium
All rights reserved

**Library of Congress
Cataloging-in-Publication
Data**
Roden, Katie, 1970-
Farming / by Katie Roden :
illustrated by James Field,
Stephen Sweet
p. cm. — (Then and now)
Includes index.
Summary: Charts the
development of agriculture
from the Stone Age to the
present.
ISBN 0-7613-0493-2
1. Agriculture—History—
Juvenile literature.
[1.Agriculture—History.]
I. Field, James, 1959- ill.
II. Stephen Sweet ill.
III. Title. IV. Series: Then and
now (Brookfield, Conn.)
S519.S73 1996   96-9837
630'.9—dc20   CIP AC

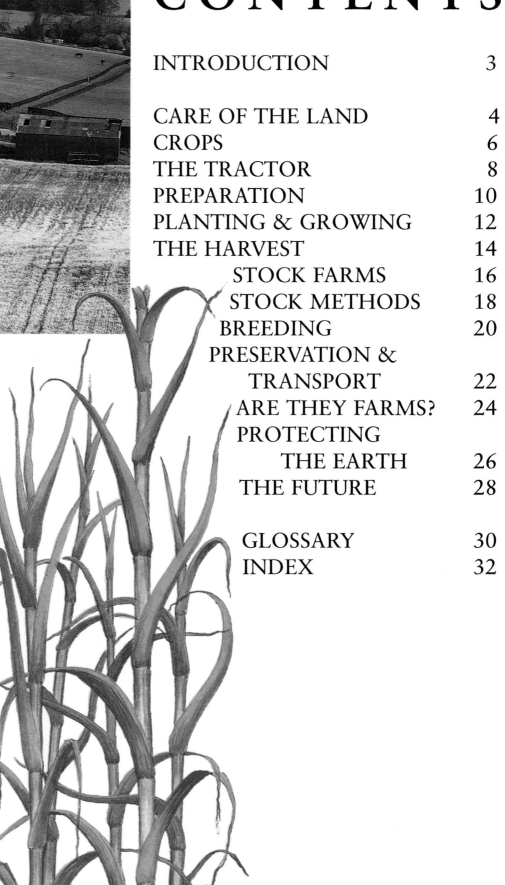

CONTENTS

INTRODUCTION

Farming has existed for almost as long as the human race itself. The first farmers experimented with planting seeds, herding and rearing animals, and preparing the ground. They knew little about caring for the soil or breeding the best types of animals. Today, scientists strive constantly to produce better livestock and plants, while the conservation of the soil and the Earth's other natural resources is an important issue worldwide. This book describes the origins and development of many of the farming methods that are used around the world.

Farming as we know it faces a future of great change. After thousands of years, and especially after heavy use in the 20th century, the Earth's resources are becoming exhausted. New farming methods must be found in order to restore and improve them. The latest technology is now being used to develop new techniques, including underwater farming and cultivation in space. But the reason that farming is so important has remained the same throughout history: to meet the world's increasing need for food, clothing, fuel, wood, medicine, and a wide range of other vital products.

CARE OF THE LAND

Early people rarely took care of their farmland. With few mouths to feed, they were unaware that land must be looked after to grow massive amounts of food.

Over the centuries, the world's population has increased, taking up more land to live on. This means that less land is available for farming. As a result, the available land has to be looked after very carefully to grow enough food. Water must be made available through irrigation systems such as ditches. As certain crops take nutrients out of the soil, these nutrients have to be replaced to stop the soil from becoming useless.

GUARDIANS OF THE SOIL
Many early people worshiped gods of agriculture and fertility and performed ceremonies to please them and so ensure a good harvest. This Mesopotamian seal-stone (c. 2900 B.C., *above*) shows the worship of a grain god.

FLOODING THE LAND
Some crops, such as rice, need a lot of water to grow. To create a rice paddy (field), channels are dug in the mud *(left)*. The ground is plowed, flooded, and then seedlings are planted.

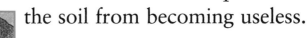

WASTE NOT, WANT NOT

One of the oldest, most efficient systems of land irrigation was developed by the ancient Egyptians. Once a year, the Nile River would flood, swamping the dry farmland on its banks. The Egyptians dug deep ditches beside their fields *(below)*. The floodwater would flow into these channels. It was stored and used to water the fields when the Nile was low.

SURFACE DRAINAGE
This ancient method *(top)* uses ditches which carry excess water away from the soil, so that it does not flood the land. It is used on flat ground, where water cannot flow away, and in areas of high rainfall. Surface drains are useful for types of soil that do not absorb water well, such as clay. But they also get in the way of people and machinery!

THE ROMANS

The Roman Empire (753 B.C.-A.D. 476) covered many countries, from Africa and Asia to northern Europe. As its armies advanced, they discovered and passed on many farming techniques. Some of these, including crop rotation, are still in use today.

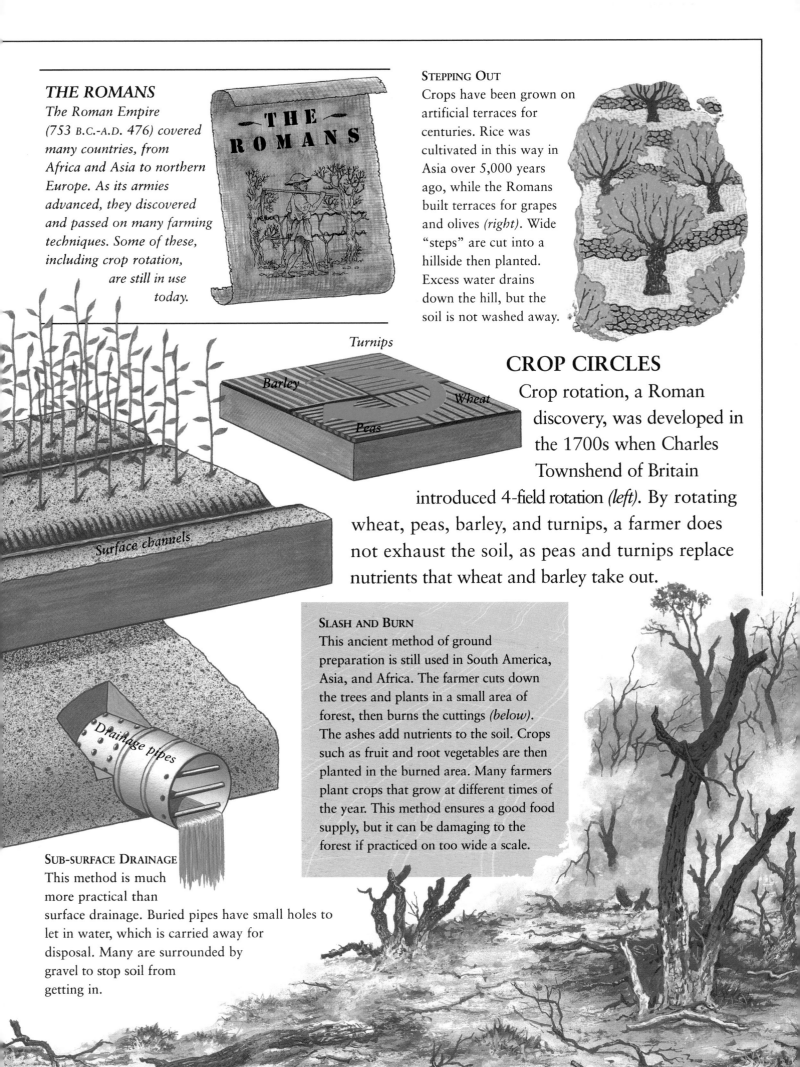

STEPPING OUT

Crops have been grown on artificial terraces for centuries. Rice was cultivated in this way in Asia over 5,000 years ago, while the Romans built terraces for grapes and olives (right). Wide "steps" are cut into a hillside then planted. Excess water drains down the hill, but the soil is not washed away.

Turnips

Barley

Peas

Wheat

CROP CIRCLES

Crop rotation, a Roman discovery, was developed in the 1700s when Charles Townshend of Britain introduced 4-field rotation (left). By rotating wheat, peas, barley, and turnips, a farmer does not exhaust the soil, as peas and turnips replace nutrients that wheat and barley take out.

Surface channels

Drainage pipes

SUB-SURFACE DRAINAGE

This method is much more practical than surface drainage. Buried pipes have small holes to let in water, which is carried away for disposal. Many are surrounded by gravel to stop soil from getting in.

SLASH AND BURN

This ancient method of ground preparation is still used in South America, Asia, and Africa. The farmer cuts down the trees and plants in a small area of forest, then burns the cuttings (below). The ashes add nutrients to the soil. Crops such as fruit and root vegetables are then planted in the burned area. Many farmers plant crops that grow at different times of the year. This method ensures a good food supply, but it can be damaging to the forest if practiced on too wide a scale.

CROPS

Over thousands of years, peoples around the world have discovered which plants are safe to eat, which plants can be grown in certain regions, and how to harvest crops successfully.

Today, technology has greatly improved the production and increased the quality of crops. The techniques used include combining the best qualities of different plants and developing fertilizers and pesticides. These have given us an amazing variety of fruit, vegetables, and other food crops.

CORN
Corn was first grown in South America. The crop was so important that it even had its own gods, as shown by this statue *(above)* made by the Mochica people of Peru.

THE FIRST FARMERS
In about 9000 B.C., people realized that plants grew from seeds and could be cultivated. They began to gather and plant a variety of seeds, to ensure that they had a constant food supply.

Neolithic sickle

EARLY ALCOHOL
The cultivation of grapes to make wine dates from at least 5000 BC. Christians spread wine-making methods, many of which are still used today.

PROTECTIVE SYSTEMS
Care for crops does not end with harvesting. On banana plantations, each bunch is cut down and wrapped carefully to protect it *(right)*.

CEREALS
Ancient Egyptian paintings show wheat harvests *(above)*. Cereal farming methods changed little until the invention of the seed drill *(see page 12)*, when crops could be sown more efficiently.

SWEET CROPS
Cane sugar *(left)* was grown on Pacific islands over 8,000 years ago. Cultivation had spread to China and Europe by A.D. 636. European settlers planted cane in America and took it to Australia. In 1799, it was discovered that beets produced sugar. Today, nearly 40% of the world's sugar comes from beets.

A NICE CUP OF TEA

In Chinese legend, tea-drinking was invented by Emperor Shang Yeng in 2737 B.C. The first record of tea-drinking in China dates from A.D. 350. By A.D. 600, it had become a Japanese custom. Tea was first taken to Europe by Dutch merchants in 1610. Today, there are vast plantations in China, Indonesia, East Africa, India, Russia, and Japan. The best tea comes from the tender leaves at the top of the plant; these are still picked by hand.

THE POTATO

Potatoes were first grown by the Incas in South America and were taken to Europe in the 16th century. Although early potatoes were picked by hand, today's crops are gathered using harvesters. Sweet potatoes, which also came from South America, are grown a lot in tropical countries.

A FRUITY HISTORY

Using scientific techniques *(see pages 20-21)*, fruit growers can now produce plants that grow without the care they needed during the Middle Ages *(above)*. For example, until recently the British cherry crop was devastated by starlings, which could eat the fruit growing in tall, unprotected trees. Since then, growers have developed a smaller cherry tree which can be covered easily to protect the fruit.

THE COCONUT

This is probably one of the world's most versatile plants! The trees provide wood for building, leaves that can be used for roofing or hats, and sap for sugar, vinegar, and alcohol. The flesh and milk of the nut are nutritious foods.

THE COCONUT

THE TERRIBLE CONSEQUENCE

After the 16th century, Europeans transported slaves from Africa to work on their farms. Life for these slaves on the plantations was appalling *(right)*. The workers were chained and beaten, and had little food or water.

7

THE TRACTOR

The tractor is one of the most important inventions in the history of farming, and today there are about 26 million in use around the world. The earliest tractors were powered by steam. They were extremely powerful, but awkward to drive. Today, tractors vary in size and shape, from massive monsters, powered by turbo-diesel engines, to lighter, multi-purpose models. Around the farm, the tractor performs two roles: pulling loads efficiently and powering other equipment.

STRONG AS AN OX
The word "tractor" comes from "traction" (pulling) and it is this feature which makes the vehicle so important. It has more strength than the oxen or horses used in traditional farming methods *(above)*, and it can work steadily without resting.

THE AGE OF STEAM

Built in the mid-19th century, steam-powered machines were known as "traction engines" *(right)*. These engines were used to power a number of machines, including threshers. The traction engine would pull the thresher into the fields and power it while it threshed the crop.

1870s

THE STEAM ENGINE
Steam engines *(left)* were operated by the expansion of steam, which pushed pistons up and down. Oil, wood, or coal were burned in a furnace to heat water in a boiler, which then produced the steam.

PULLING POWER
Tractors can pull an amazing array of equipment *(below)*, such as plows and harrows. They can also be used to power mowing machines and spray pumps.

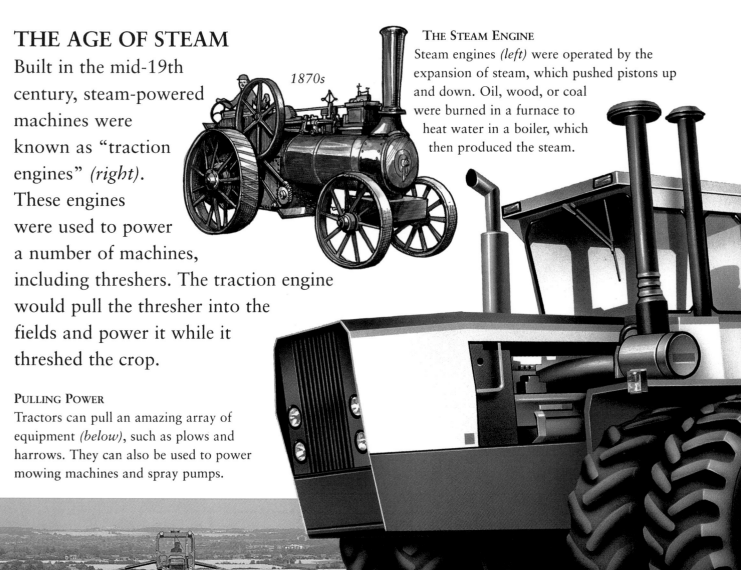

8

LIGHTNESS OR STRENGTH?
The early tractors *(right)* were small and light. However, they were not really powerful enough to pull the large machinery found around today's farms.

GASOLINE POWER

In the 1890s, the first efficient gasoline engines, built into the tractor frame, were introduced in the United States. The all-purpose tractor *(left)* was invented in the 1920s. This could power all kinds of equipment and quickly replaced steam engines and animals on almost all American farms, then around the world. Modern tractors are run using diesel rather than gasoline, as they are more efficient.

HARRY FERGUSON

HENRY GEORGE FERGUSON (1884-1960)
Ferguson was a British engineer. In 1908, he built a plane and became the first Briton to fly. But he is most famous for the Ferguson farm tractor, with hydraulic linkage powered by water) which gave more control and stability. This helped to speed up the mechanization of farming worldwide.

TRACTOR FEATURES
The most important features of a modern tractor are those which allow it to pull and power other equipment. These include: the **drawbar,** to which machinery is attached; the **power takeoff** which powers the equipment pulled by the tractor; and the **hydraulic system** which can alter the position of equipment attached to the tractor.

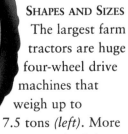

World-famous 'ALL-BRITISH'
Saunderson
UNIVERSAL **TRACTOR**
As supplied to
HIS MAJESTY THE KING
and His Royal Highness
The Prince of Wales.
Awarded FIRST PRIZE SILVER MEDAL of
the Royal Agricultural Society of England.
Complete with Power Driving Pulley,
Winding Drum and 50 yds. Steel Cable.
THE SAUNDERSON TRACTOR & IMP
Elstow Works.

THE MANUFACTURERS
The first tractor-making companies manufactured only one type or size of vehicle, such as this "Saunderson Tractor" *(left)*. Industrial technology now allows manufacturers to make a range of tractors, designed to suit different farming needs *(below)*.

SHAPES AND SIZES
The largest farm tractors are huge four-wheel drive machines that weigh up to 7.5 tons *(left)*. More usually, tractors are two-wheel drive and can weigh as little as 1.4 tons.

PREPARATION

Thousands of years ago, people realized that plants grow better in loose soil, which lets in more air and water. They began to turn the soil over with sticks, bones, and rocks.

About 8,000 years ago, there was a breakthrough – the invention of the *ard*, a hand-pulled plow made from a large, forked branch. One prong was sharpened then charred in a fire to make it harder. As this hardened point was pulled through the soil it made a furrow. *Ards* are still used in some countries today.

FEEDING THE GROUND
Before the invention of the plow, early people used sticks to make holes for air and water *(above)*.

BEASTS OF BURDEN
By 3000 B.C., Egyptian and Mesopotamian farmers used oxen to pull plows *(top)*, thus increasing the areas which could be planted. Roman explorers took this method back to Europe.

THE HORSE ARRIVES
Oxen *(below)* were gradually replaced by horses for plowing. By A.D. 900, the horse-drawn plow was common in many parts of the world. At the start of the Industrial Revolution, in about 1765, James Small of Britain designed and made the first cast-iron plow.

Moldboard plows (left) *have been used since the Middle Ages, as they are the most versatile type.*

INNOVATIONS

Small's plow was redesigned in the United States in 1830 by James Oliver. He divided the plow into parts that could be mass-produced and bought individually. Today, many farms use a cultivator instead of a plow to aerate (put air into) the soil. Instead of turning the soil over, this piece of equipment, pulled behind a tractor, uses a series of long spikes which dig deep into the ground.

POWER PLOWING
By the early 19th century, steam-powered plows were being developed. Each plow was attached by ropes to two steam engines *(right)*.

One engine would pull the plow across the field. When it reached the first engine, the plow was moved to the site of the next furrow to be dug. The driver of the second engine wound in the rope, pulling the plow back.

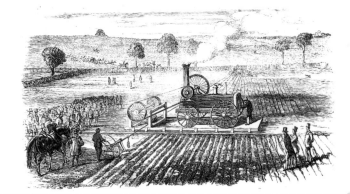

JOHN DEERE (1804-1886)
Deere, a U.S. blacksmith, designed various plows with a partner. But he won fame in 1840 when he invented the cast-steel plow, which made it easier to turn heavy soil. He also made a "sulky" plow with wheels and a seat.

DEERE'S PLOW

This tractor is pulling a plow which is fitted with a moldboard cutting tool. This buries old crop remains in the soil as it plows the field.

TYPES OF PLOWS
Because soils vary, different designs of cutting tools are needed on plows.
The main cutting tools are: **moldboard** – the most widely used type, which buries waste matter from old crops; **disk** – for sticky or tough soil; **rotary** – mixes old crop material with the soil; **drill** – lifts the soil without turning it.

MODERN PLOWING

Both traditional and modern methods are used to plow fields today. Farmers in developing countries still use walking plows, pulled by animals, as machinery is expensive. Most farmers in developed countries use a tractor plow made from steel or iron *(left)* or a cultivator, which requires an extremely powerful tractor to pull it.

PLANTING & GROWING

Until the early 18th century, sowing seeds was done by hand. But hand-sowing was not very precise. Precious seeds were thrown out at random by the sower and some could easily land on bad soil. In the late 1800s, a hand-held sowing machine, or "seed fiddle," was invented. This allowed the sower to spread seeds more accurately and easily. Today, tractor-pulled seed drills are used.

THE INGENIOUS INCAS
Most Inca people of South America lived in rural, agricultural communities and so developed highly efficient farming methods. They used foot-plows tipped with hard wood or bronze to turn the soil, and digging sticks to help their planting *(above)*.

DIBBLE AWAY!
Digging sticks, or "dibblers" *(above)*, were pushed into the ground to make a single hole. A seed could then be planted, making sowing more accurate and efficient.

NO MORE BACKACHE!
A revolution in sowing came in 1701, when an English farmer, Jethro Tull, invented the seed drill *(above)* – the first farm machine with moving parts. The drill had a "coulter" (cutter) to carve a "drill" (furrow) in the soil. The grain was stored in a seed box and pushed out by a rotating brush. It fell into a hole, down a funnel, and into the furrow. The drill operator would tread soil into the furrow to bury the grain. The size of the hole could be altered to sow different varieties of seeds.

RESTRICTED

LOST HILLS
FLYING SERVICE, INC.

AGWAGON

N9335R

PAUL MÜLLER

INTENSIVE GROWTH

As global demand for food has increased, technology has been used to improve production. Today, huge commercial greenhouses, some of them solar powered, are used to grow crops out of season, such as tomatoes, cucumbers, and even flowers. Many have computer controls to alter the heat, fertilizer, light, the amount of water given to the plants, and the humidity of the air.

PAUL HERMANN MÜLLER (1899-1965)
Müller, a Swiss chemist, discovered the insecticide properties of the chemical DDT in 1939. He won a Nobel Prize in 1948. But DDT is now banned in many places.

WHAT A PEST!
The late 1800s and early 1900s saw the development of chemicals to control diseases and pests, such as weevils *(left)*. But in the 1950s, many, including DDT, were found to harm the environment. Today, alternatives are being developed.

SWARM!
The locust is feared in Africa and the Middle East. Locusts have huge appetites – a single insect will eat its own weight in food every day. If a large number are crowded together, they form a swarm of up to a billion insects. Wherever they settle, they eat – a swarm can eat 20,000 tons of plants in a day, making locusts disastrous for crop farmers.

FERTILE SOIL

Fertilizers have been used for thousands of years. At first, they came from natural sources, such as manure. By the 1900s, botanists knew that plants needed certain chemicals to thrive, and so made artificial fertilizers containing them. Other plants can be used to replace nutrients. Beans and peas are grown with rubber trees to feed the soil.

CROP SPRAYING
Crop-spraying planes and helicopters are used on large farms to scatter pesticide or fertilizers. A farmer can quickly deliver a precise amount of chemicals over a very wide area in a short space of time.

Clappers

STRAW PEOPLE
Scarecrows *(right)* date from the 18th century. Until then, birds were kept off growing crops by children, often standing alone in the fields, who shouted at the birds and used clappers *(above)* or rattles. Today, mechanical bird scarers are used. These emit high-pitched noises and the sound of gunshots.

13

THE HARVEST

Traditionally, crops were harvested by hand *(left)*, either by picking them from trees and bushes or by cutting them with scythes *(right)*. This is still the case for some crops, such as tea, grapes, olives, and rice. However, massive combine harvesters usually do all the jobs needed to gather a variety of plants. They can do the work of hundreds of people in a fraction of the time and in all conditions.

ANCIENT HARVESTS
Images of the harvest are found among all ancient civilizations. They were often put in places of worship, as offerings to the gods in return for a good crop the next year. Many religions still hold harvest ceremonies.

Bronze Age sickle

CUTTING THE CORN
Scythes and sickles have been used since ancient times. The scythe dates from at least the Roman era and was used to cut a crop in a single, strong stroke. The sickle *(above)*, a smaller, lighter version, has been used since prehistoric times. Sickles are still used widely today, despite the development of machinery, because they are cheap to make and easy to use.

Iron Age sickle

Handle

THE SCYTHE
This consists of a long, straight handle made of wood with a metal blade, supported by a metal *grassnail*. Originally, scythes were sharpened with a *straik (below)* – a piece of pitted wood smeared with mutton fat and soft or stony sand, depending on the sharpness needed.

Grassnail

Straik

THRESHING
Threshing (separating) grains from stalks and winnowing (blowing) the husks from the grains were done by hand until 1780, when Andrew Meickle of Scotland built the first machine. Early threshers worked by horse power. The horses walked on a treadmill *(right)* to turn the machine. This was replaced in the mid-1800s by steam-powered engines.

FARMING... ON A MASSIVE SCALE!
China grows the most crops in the world – about 19% of the Earth's total production. This is followed by the United States with about 14%, then Russia. The most efficient harvest ever gathered was collected by an agricultural team in Britain. With a single combine harvester, they gathered 352 tons of wheat in only eight hours in August 1990!

1

14

PATRICK BELL (1801-1869) Bell, a Scottish clergyman, invented a mechanical reaper in 1827, but it did not catch on quickly. In 1834, Cyrus Hall McCormick of Virginia saw one of the reapers. He produced a similar machine adapted into a combined reaper and binder.

PATRICK BELL

MULTI-PURPOSE MACHINES

In the early 1900s, work began on a combined reaper and thresher. It had an engine which worked the moving parts *(above)*. Today, combines come in many sizes, to suit different crops and fields. They have special attachments to harvest crops other than cereals, such as soybeans and cotton. Some are designed to harvest unusual crops like trees or potatoes. Most are self-propelled, although the smallest may be pulled by tractors.

HOW THE COMBINE WORKS
1. A cutting bar cuts the stalks with rotating paddles.
2. The stalks fall onto a platform and are carried by a feeder to a threshing drum. A revolving cylinder separates the grain from the stalks, then the stalks are discarded and used for straw.
3. The grain passes through sieves and the husks are blown away by a fan.
4. The grain is fed into a tank. From here it is poured into trucks and taken away for storage.

4

STOCK FARMS

Prehistoric peoples lived as hunter-gatherers – hunting animals and collecting plants and berries for food. Certain people still practice this lifestyle in the more remote parts of the world. However, about 9,000 years ago, the herding and breeding of animals, such as sheep and cattle, were developed in the Middle East. These provided people with a regular supply of milk, eggs, and meat.

Today, farmers breed an amazing array of animals to keep pace with the increase in demand for food. These range from dairy cattle, fish, and pigs to llamas, ostriches, and even crocodiles.

STONE AGE HERDERS
This 5,000-year-old rock painting *(above)*, in the Sahara Desert of Africa, shows cattle herding. At that time, parts of the Sahara were grassland. The herders may have traveled up to 1,500 miles (2,500 km) in search of fodder.

THE FIRST COWBOYS
By 1500 B.C., herders were using horses and camels to help to control their animals. Nomadic farmers like Arab warrior-herders *(above)* could now travel even further. Modern herders are more likely to use motorcycles!

NOMADIC HERDING

This was the original method of stock farming. Nomadic herders would allow small herds of animals like goats or cattle to wander freely as they searched for fresh pastures. This ensured that the herd was always well fed and the farmer had a constant supply of meat. Nomadic herding still occurs. For example, the Sami of Lapland travel with herds of reindeer.

Sumerian cattle herders, c. 3000 B.C.

16

Egyptian goose farmers

A PIGGY HISTORY

Wild pigs lived in Europe up to 6 million years ago. During the Stone Age, early people began to tame and breed them. They were taken to North and South America in the 1500s and to Australia and New Zealand in the 18th century.

POULTRY

Chickens were tamed in prehistoric times and were bred in China over 3,000 years ago. Turkeys came from Mexico and were taken by explorers back to Europe via Turkey. Geese were kept in Egypt over 4,000 years ago *(above)* and were later reared by the Greeks and Romans.

RANCHING

In places with poor-quality grazing, such as Australia, New Zealand, the southern U.S., and South America, stock farms may be spread over vast areas, known as ranches. The animals can wander freely in search of food. They are rounded up *(below)* only when it is time for shearing or dipping *(see pages 18-19)* or if they are to be sold.

ELIZABETH MACARTHUR (1766-1850) MacArthur emigrated from England to Australia in 1789. She introduced merino sheep to the country and bred them to produce the finest possible wool. This formed the basis of the Australian wool industry, which is one of the country's most profitable trades today.

Holstein-Friesian cattle

THE HISTORICAL COW

For thousands of years, water buffalo have been used in Asia for plowing and other heavy tasks. The Romans were the first to breed cattle selectively. In 100 B.C., the first specialized dairy cow – the Holstein-Friesian *(above)* – was introduced. This type of breeding continued throughout the Middle Ages. Today, farmers keep a wide variety of cattle for both their meat and their milk. These include Jersey, Brahman, and Hereford cattle.

FARMS AS FAR AS THE EYE CAN SEE

Australia, with its enormous tracts of land, has the largest stock farms in the world. The country's biggest cattle ranch, at Anna Creek, covers an amazing 11,600 square miles (30,000 square kilometers). The world's largest sheep ranch, in South Australia, covers 4,080 square miles (10,567 square kilometers).

17

STOCK METHODS

HANDY MILKING
Milking was first done by hand *(below)*, and is still done this way in parts of the world. In ancient Babylon, India, and Egypt, each family kept a cow to provide milk.

Animal farming has changed a great deal in the last 10,000 years. The treatment of animals has improved the production of meat, milk, eggs, and wool (some cows can now produce over 1,500 gallons (6,000 liters) of milk a year!). Animals can be protected from illness, allowing them to live longer. However, some modern methods of animal rearing are causing concern.

THE MILKING MACHINE

It is not quite clear when the milking machine was invented, as many designs were proposed over the years. In 1878, Anna Baldwin, an American farmer, invented a machine that obtained milk by suction. But milking machines only became successful after 1898, when J. Wallis from Scotland invented the pulsator. This mimicked the sucking action of the calf, and is still used today.

POOR COWS!
Early machines *(above, 1862)* were not invented with much concern for the cow! The udders were often squeezed extremely hard in order to force out the milk.

Pulsator

LOUIS PASTEUR (1822-1895) Pasteur, a French scientist, discovered that diseases are spread by bacteria. He showed that cows and sheep could be protected from anthrax by being injected with some of the bacteria. By keeping animals alive longer, his work revolutionized farming.

MAKING MILK
Today's milking parlors *(above)* are kept very clean. After the cow has been milked, the "raw milk" must be pasteurized to remove any harmful bacteria. Once this is done, the milk can be turned into a variety of products, such as yogurt and butter.

A CONTROVERSIAL ISSUE
The growth of intensive farming has caused great debate. Conditions in fattening houses and battery farms are often poor and cramped. They are not good for the physical and mental health of the animals or for the quality of their produce.

INTENSIVE FARMING
This method was developed in the 20th century in response to an increasing demand for food. As many animals as possible are reared in the space available. Pigs are raised in fattening houses *(left)*, while battery farms contain thousands of chickens *(above left)*. Both are given special food to improve production. Opponents prefer free-range farming *(above right)*, in which animals are kept in more open spaces.

DINNERTIME
Special feeds can increase milk and meat production. The amount given to each animal is controlled. Some farms have links to computers at agricultural colleges, which tell them what quantities to use.

ANIMAL AILMENTS
There are many types of diseases, but the most common are mastitis, brucellosis, foot and mouth, tsetse fly, and liver rot. The new disease of BSE, caught from contaminated cattle feed, is spreading in Britain. Parasites are usually controlled by dipping animals in insecticide.

SHEEP MANAGEMENT
Originally found wild in the mountains of central Asia, sheep have been carefully bred over the centuries. There are now over 800 breeds. The sheep are sheared each year to obtain their wool, and are dipped regularly in insecticide to kill parasites. Traditionally, sheep were sheared using hand shears. Today's shearers use electric clippers. A good shearer, like those on the Australian sheep stations *(right)*, can shear over 200 sheep in a single day.

RAWHIDE!
A year on a cattle ranch begins in fall, when some of the cattle are sold. Preparation for winter involves buying cattle feed which is given to the remaining herd when it snows. Calves are born in spring and they are rounded up and branded. They are grazed through the summer.

BREEDING

Since farming began, people have looked for ways of breeding better types of animals and plants, to improve their yield and to produce varieties suited to specific purposes. In 1700, Robert Bakewell of England invented a method of improving the quality of livestock by breeding animals with desirable characteristics. This has led to a huge variety of animals, each bred for specific needs – for example, Charolais cattle are reared only for their meat.

New varieties of plants are being developed all the time: to provide more or better-quality food for humans and animals; to grow faster; to be disease-resistant; or to survive in harsh climates.

RIDING POWER
Horses have been selectively bred for centuries. Arab horses *(above)* were swift and strong. They were taken to Europe after A.D. 900 and used to breed high-quality horses. Arabs are still valuable today.

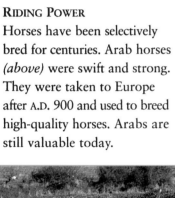

BREEDING TECHNIQUES
A cross-breed is produced by the mating of animals from different breeds, such as two types of cow *(left)*. Pure-breeding is the mating of the best animals from the same breed.

ARTIFICIAL INSEMINATION

This technique, developed in the mid-20th century, has made selective breeding easier, as the animals do not have to meet. The farmer can control when the cow is ready to become pregnant. When this happens, the farmer buys bull's semen (the fluid which contains sperm). This semen is placed inside the cow, where the sperm fertilizes the egg. Using artificial insemination, one bull can be mated to more than 3,000 cows every year!

A LIVESTOCK LEGEND
By far the heaviest cattle weight ever recorded was that of Mount Katahdin, a Durham-Holstein cross, in Maine. His weight rose to 5,000 pounds (2,267 kg)! In comparison, an average bull weighs about 1,980 lb (900 kg).

A PERFECT COW?
The Aberdeen Angus *(above)* has been specially bred for the quality of its meat. It can also adapt to a variety of climates.

TIME STANDS STILL

These tomatoes and barley *(left)* have been developed with genes that delay the ripening process. This means that they can be transported over long distances and stay fresh. It also increases the time that produce can be displayed in stores.

GREGOR MENDEL (1822-1884)

Mendel was a monk with an interest in botany. He found that the genes of an organism (its basic features) are inherited by each generation and can be altered by selective breeding. His work formed the basis of modern genetics.

GREGOR MENDEL

USES OF SCIENCE

By the 1960s, the science of genetics was firmly established and was producing animals (including fish, *left*) and crops with much higher yields. For example, average corn yields in the United States increased from 170 bushels per acre in the 1920s to 720 bushels per acre in the 1980s.

THE TECHNIQUE

To alter the cells of an organism, two genes with the desired characteristics are split and combined to produce a new gene. This is placed into a cell, which multiplies to form a new organism. Each of its cells contains the altered genetic information.

STRAWBERRY FIELDS FOREVER

The strawberries of today are very different from their ancestors! Small, wild strawberries *(above left)* were first cultivated by the Romans. It was not until the 18th century that they were combined with another variety from Chile. This produced the larger variety that we eat today.

SUPER PLANTS!

Genetic techniques have produced a wide range of "super plants." Grafting (joining parts of two plants to make one plant) can also determine a plant's characteristics. For example, it can produce seedless fruits, such as grapes, and trees that can bear more than one type of apple. Scientists have also developed bacteria with altered genes, which act as pesticides when they are placed on crops.

PRESERVATION & TRANSPORT

For centuries, food producers and farmers have faced a major problem – how to transport produce while keeping it as fresh as when it was gathered. And this continues to be a problem, especially as large amounts of food are shipped worldwide. Prehistoric peoples dried food by laying it out in the sun *(below)* and later with fire. In winter, it was put outside to be preserved by the ice and wind. Today, some food, such as bacon *(right)*, is coated with chemicals to mimic the effect of smoking *(see below)*.

SALTY STORY
Salting has been used for thousands of years. Produce is dried by the salt and so does not spoil. Fresh food was put in barrels of salt for sea journeys. Later, chemicals were added to the salt. Salt curing is still carried out, often on an industrial scale.

A CHILLY STORY

In colder countries, people built ice houses or cellars in their homes, in which food could be preserved by the cold. It was not until 1925 that Clarence Birdseye, an American businessman, invented a method of freezing foods in small quantities that were easy to sell and transport. Modern electric freezers can freeze food quickly, keeping it fresh for a long time.

SMOKING
Ancient people preserved meat or fish by smoking it over fires. Different types of wood produced different smoke, which altered the taste of the meat. Smoked meat and fish are still delicacies.

CAN IT!
In the 1700s, meat was sealed into glass jars and heated, making it edible for several weeks. This was the basis of modern canning.

Tin cans, 1835

DRYING METHODS
There are various drying techniques: **sun** – food is placed in the sun *(right)*; **freeze** with dry ice; **tray** with hot air; **spray** with air and liquid; **pulse-combustion** with sound and heat waves.

CLARENCE
BIRDSEYE

***CLARENCE BIRDSEYE
(1886-1956)***
Birdseye is best remembered for his development of packaged frozen food, and for his companies General Seafoods and Birdseye Frosted Foods. But he was also the inventor of about 300 other objects, including infrared heat lamps.

THE TRANSPORT DEBATE

The live transport of animals is the best way to ensure the freshness of the meat on arrival, but the methods used have caused great controversy. Animals are often carried in overcrowded trucks, without enough air, water or rest, especially in countries with few regulations.

INTO THE NUCLEAR AGE
The newest development in the preservation of food is the use of gamma rays (a type of radiation similar to X rays, *left*). The rays destroy the bacteria that contribute to the ripening of produce such as potatoes and other fruit and vegetables. This ripening of the food eventually leads to it going bad.

The destruction of the bacteria slows down the ripening process and allows the produce to be shipped over long distances without rotting before arrival. Gamma radiation is effective, but the risks it might pose to human health are still unknown.

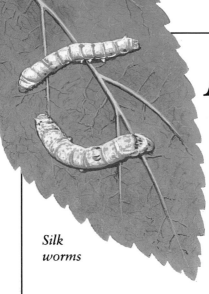

Silk worms

ARE THEY FARMS?

As global demand for food and other goods has increased, people have had to turn to new farming methods – from breeding unusual animals, such as crocodiles, for alternative sources of meat, to growing trees and other plants for fuel. For example, huge regions of Brazil have been given up to grow sugar plants, which may be turned into alcohol and then used to run cars.

"Wind farms" consist of thousands of wind turbines which convert the power of the wind into electricity, saving the Earth's precious fossil fuel resources.

A CLOSELY GUARDED SECRET
In Chinese legend, silk was discovered in 2700 B.C. and was kept secret for 2,000 years. Making silk has not changed much since then. Even in the biggest farms, the cocoons of the larvae *(top left)* are unwrapped by hand to get fine strands of silk.

LLAMA FARMING
Llamas, from South America, are wool-bearers that can live in almost any conditions. Llama farming is now a big business.

HEADS IN THE SAND
In the late 1800s, ostrich plumes became fashionable accessories in Europe *(left)*. As a result, the species was almost wiped out. Ostrich farms soon sprang up in northern and southern Africa, the United States, Europe, and Australia. By 1918, however, fashions had changed and the plumes were no longer wanted. Ostriches continue to be farmed for leather, meat, and eggs.

RAPESEED
Rapeseed, a flowering herb, is farmed in Europe, New Zealand, and Asia. It is becoming an important crop because its seeds produce oil. This oil can be used for cooking and to make soap and fuel. It is also used to make cheap feed for livestock.

RUBBER

Native North Americans tapped wild rubber trees for latex to make toys and shoes. Rubber cultivation developed in the 1700s. When the car was invented, worldwide demand for rubber increased. Latex is still tapped by hand.

A FISHY TALE

Aquaculture (fish farming) has been practiced in China for at least 4,000 years, and China still produces the most fish. Today, aquaculture is a good alternative to the overfishing of the seas. All sorts of sea plants and creatures are farmed: **mollusks** such as oysters for food; **seaweeds** for food, fertilizer, and animal fodder; **crustaceans** such as lobsters for food; **fish**, both freshwater and marine, such as salmon, for food and natural oils.

A STING IN THE TAIL

Honey has been used as food since the Stone Age, when early peoples took it from the nests of wild bees. Today, bees are also used on the Great Plains, to increase the amount of plants for cattle fodder. Huge mobile hives tour the country. At certain places, the trucks are opened and the bees fly out to feed on the plants, carrying pollen and thus fertilizing them.

INSECTS

In many areas, insects are used as food and some are seen as delicacies, such as the honey-ant of Australia (right). Insects are cheap and nutritious, yet to some people the idea of eating them is revolting. But farming them might be one way to increase the world's food supply.

COTTON

Cotton was first cultivated by the Persians about 5,000 years ago. It was taken to Europe by Alexander the Great's army in the 4th century B.C., and spread around the world. In 1793, Eli Whitney invented the cotton gin *(right)*. This removed seeds, saving hours of labor. Today, there is a wide variety of cotton-picking equipment *(left)*, but it is still harvested by hand in places such as India and Thailand.

PROTECTING THE EARTH

The 20th century has seen a vast increase in the use of the world's limited natural resources. Without careful management they will soon become exhausted.

Overfishing has led to a lack of fish stocks in the oceans, and land that has been used for agriculture for thousands of years is now becoming infertile. The deserts are increasing in size, as millions of trees are cut down and more animals are grazed on the land. Yet more food is needed to feed the increasing population of the world.

ANCIENT IRRIGATION
The *shaduf (above)*, used in ancient Egypt, was one of the earliest irrigation tools. Traditional methods of cultivation are being turned to again, in an effort to stop overfarming.

THE DYING SEAS

The 20th-century fishing industry operates on a vast scale, catching and processing millions of fish every year. But this means that in many marine waters, such as the northern Atlantic Ocean, fish stocks have been greatly reduced. Governments are now imposing controlled fishing zones and limits on the numbers of fish caught by fishing vessels *(above right)*, while large-scale aquaculture *(see page 25)* is another step toward a solution.

ENDING EROSION
Terraces *(see page 5)* are now being built in an effort to prevent the loss of precious nutrients from the soil *(left)*. In Africa, the spread of the desert is being restrained by networks of fences and new trees and plants, while walls are often built across valleys to stop the soil from being washed away.

26

WATERING THE LAND

While the ancient system of ditches and canals *(right)* is still used in many areas, large-scale mechanical irrigation is now common on the world's bigger farms. Spinning water pipes can throw large jets of water over crops. Where water is scarce, drip irrigators give a carefully controlled supply of water to each individual plant, or pipes deliver a precise amount of water when required. In dry countries, such as Israel, large areas of land that were once barren have now become fertile, thanks to careful irrigation.

THOUGHTLESS FISHING

Huge trawl nets, used in large-scale sea fishing, can trap millions of fish at a time. But they also catch many other creatures, most of which cannot be eaten.

THE MAYA This Central American civilization flourished in the third to eighth centuries A.D. However, from the ninth century onward their civilization declined rapidly, and by A.D. 1000 it had disappeared completely. The reason for this is not really clear, but the most likely explanation is that the Maya simply overfarmed their land as their population grew. This led to infertility of the soil and failure of their food crops on a massive scale.

THE DUST BOWL

During the late 1930s, 8 million acres of land in the United States were ruined by a series of dust storms that destroyed crops. The storms were caused by poor farming practices. By turning vast areas of grassland over to growing wheat, the farmers did not protect the soil from the wind. The result was one of the worst ecological disasters ever seen.

ORGANIC FARMS

Organic farming uses traditional methods to prevent pollution. Farmers plant different crops in the same field to keep the soil fertile *(right)*. They also use natural fertilizers, like manure and compost, and natural pesticides, such as planting onions among carrots to prevent carrot-fly.

THE GIANTS OF IRRIGATION

In countries where water is plentiful, huge, moving crop sprayers are used *(below)*. They have soft tires so that they do not damage the soil or crops, and they spray a thin film of water as they travel across the fields.

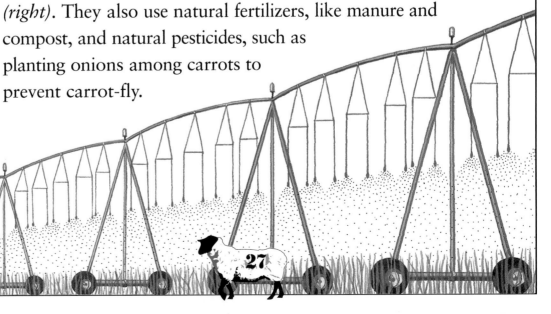

27

THE FUTURE

The balance between the amount of food that is produced and the number of mouths to feed is reaching a crisis point. Despite the huge advances made in agriculture in recent years, farmers of the future will still have to grow more food and pay closer attention to environmental concerns. Because fertile farmland is now scarce, there is a growing demand for alternative techniques, such as hydroponics *(left)* and using space-saving frames *(right)*. The most up-to-date technology is also being used to improve crop yields.

WHO NEEDS SOIL, ANYWAY? Developed in the mid-19th century, hydroponics is a method of growing plants without soil, either by placing their roots in water, nutrient solution, sand, or gravel.
The technique is useful for growing plants in places where the soil is scarce or of poor quality.

Nutrient solution

Air supply

THE BIGGEST VEGETABLES EVER! Developments in the breeding and cultivation of fruit and vegetables have led to the introduction of enormous varieties, such as pumpkins and cucumbers. Some of these plants even have inbred pesticides.

OBSERVING THE EARTH

On July 23, 1972, the satellite *Landsat 1* was launched. Its role was to photograph the Earth constantly *(above)* and send back information about the natural resources and how they are changing. This type of technology lets scientists foresee environmental problems. Action can then be taken to stop them or slow them down.

SPACE-AGE FARMING?

Biosphere 2, built in the desert near Tucson, Arizona, is a sealed mini-world, with different environments ("biomes") – oceans, forests, grasslands, marshes, and deserts. For two years, eight volunteers survived

within it, farming the land and living alongside 3,800 plant and animal species. The main goal of the project was to prove that life could be sustained there. This could lead to the development of space colonies which may be able to supply food to Earth.

BIOSPHERE BIOMES
Each biome contained a specific environment, such as an ocean, complete with coral reef, and grassland *(above)* with ants, termites, and 45 species of grass.

IMPORTANT ISSUES

A recent development in the history of farming is the importance of cruelty-free methods. More and more people protest against the mistreatment of animals on farms and in transportation worldwide *(left)*, and many governments are now imposing tighter regulations regarding the treatment of animals and birds in agriculture.

THE FOOD AND AGRICULTURE ORGANIZATION (FAO)

This agency of the United Nations was established in 1945 to improve the world's farms and to raise the standard of living of poorer people. It provides advice and help, collects and distributes information, and offers training. It remains, and will continue to be, an important weapon in the global fight against hunger.

THE FAO

GLOSSARY

Aquaculture Begun in China over 4,000 years ago; an alternative to fishing.

Aztecs A Mexican civilization of the 15th and 16th centuries A.D.; destroyed by the Spaniards.

Bananas Banana plantations first sprang up in the 1860s.

Beekeeping Begun by Stone Age people, who used hives made of logs or pots.

Breeding Selective breeding has been practiced for centuries. Breakthroughs were made after the 1700s. Today, scientists can change organisms' genes.

Camels Used for herding by 1500 B.C. In Africa and Asia, they are used for farm work and for meat, milk, and wool.

Cattle Bred over 9,000 years ago; herded by nomads. Oxen were used for farm work. There are many types, bred for specific needs.

Coconuts A versatile crop with a variety of uses, from food and milk to roofing materials and hats.

Combine harvester Developed from the combined reaper and thresher, combines were introduced in the early 1900s.

Corn A staple crop in many countries; first cultivated by Central and South American peoples.

Cotton First cultivated 5,000 years ago. The gin (1793) improved cultivation.

Crop rotation A Roman method of preserving the nutrients of the soil by planting different crops at different times.

Cultivation Preparing the land for crop-growing.

DDT DichloroDiphenylTrichloro-ethane, first used as an insecticide in 1939. But it damages animals and crops.

Drainage A part of soil preparation that takes water away from a field.

Fertilization Developed over centuries. May be natural or chemical.

Fruit-growing Early peoples cultivated wild fruit. Growers have now found ways of increasing productivity.

Fuel Natural products are farmed to provide fuel. Alcohol made from sugar in Brazil is used to power cars; rapeseed oil may also be used for fuel.

Genetics The study of how features are passed from one generation to another. Used to develop better animals and plants. It was developed in the 1800s.

Grafting Joining parts of two plants to produce one plant with desirable features.

Grapes Wild grapes were eaten by prehistoric peoples; they were cultivated for wine by at least 5000 B.C.

Greenhouse A glass building for growing plants in which conditions are carefully controlled.

Herding Nomadic herders travel over thousands of miles to find food for their animals. Today, herds are kept on farms or ranches, where farmers use motorcycles and even helicopters to round them up.

Horses Many species are bred for specific purposes – for example, Arabs were bred for speed and strength after A.D. 900. By this time, horses were also used for heavy farm work; this continued until the late 19th century, and still exists today.

Hydroponics Growing plants without soil; developed in the mid-1900s.

Incas A South American civilization, destroyed by the Spaniards in 1532.

Industrial Revolution The period spanning the late eighteenth and early nineteenth centuries, which saw rapid developments in industry.

Insects Important foods in many countries; they might provide an alternative food source for many others.

Intensive farming As many animals or plants as possible are reared in the space available. But intensive animal farming is cruel and bad for the animals' health.

Irrigation Watering the fields. The ancient Egyptians developed the first efficient system; today, many mechanical methods are also used.

Llamas Used for food, wool, and transportation in South and Central America; now farmed in other countries.

Maya A Central American civilization which flourished until the eighth century A.D., after which overfarming contributed to its decline.

Milking Done by hand until the 1800s, when machines were invented. Cows are still hand-milked in many places.

Organic farming A form of agriculture that uses only natural methods of cultivation.

Ostriches Farming began in the 19th century; it continues today for meat, leather, and eggs.

Oxen The first animals used for heavy work; replaced by horses after A.D. 900.

Pesticides Natural pesticides were used for centuries; chemical ones were invented in the late 1800s. But many are known to be harmful to people and animals.

Pigs Wild pigs existed 6 million years ago; bred since the Stone Age.

Planting Done by hand until seed drills were invented. Sowing machines are now pulled by tractors.

Plowing Sticks were first used, followed by plows pulled by humans then animals. Now many farmers use cultivators.

Potatoes First grown by the Incas, potatoes were taken to Europe then worldwide by explorers.

Poultry Reared since ancient Egyptian times and bred by the Greeks and Romans. Poultry farming is still an important food source all over the world.

Preservation Natural methods have been used since ancient times. Today, chemicals and gamma rays are also used.

Ranching Stock farming on a huge scale, usually in areas of sparse grassland such as Australia and North America.

Rapeseed Quickly becoming a major crop and the source of a variety of products.

Reaping Early tools were replaced by machines in many places after 1800.

Rice Gathered wild in Southeast Asia thousands of years ago, it was farmed by 5000 B.C.

Rubber First tapped by Native North American people. Many plantations developed, but rubber is still tapped by hand.

Sheep Bred for 9,000 years; there are over 800 breeds.

Silk Secret for 2,000 years, silk production methods have not changed much.

Slash and burn An ancient method of ground use. Trees are burned to make way for crops. Large-scale slash-and-burn farming can harm the environment.

Sugarcane was grown over 8,000 years ago and spread worldwide; in 1799, beet was found to produce sugar.

Tea Its first known use was in China in A.D. 350; it is now grown on huge plantations, but the tender leaves are still picked by hand.

Terracing Cutting "steps" into hills so that nutrients do not drain off. This has been practiced since ancient times; today it is becoming an important means of preventing soil erosion.

Threshing Separating grains from their stalks. This was done by hand until the invention of threshing machines in the 1780s; it is now done by a combine harvester.

Tractors Early types (1800s) were steam powered, followed by petrol engines. Modern ones run on diesel.

United Nations (UN) An organization of over 160 countries, founded in 1945 to promote world peace. Its agencies include the FAO.

Wind farms A means of trapping the power of the wind and converting it into electricity, by using thousands of turbines (based on traditional windmills).

INDEX

✪

Picture Credits
(t-top, m-middle, b-bottom, r-right, l-left):
Cover tlt, tr & mlt, 7tl & ml, 9mr, 15tr & 24bl – Mary Evans Picture Library. Cover tlb – Charles De Vere. Cover tm & mrt, 2, 6-7m, 16-17, 19tl, 21m, 24-25, 25t, 26, 29tl & tr – Frank Spooner Pictures. Cover mlt & mrb, 9t, 10br & back cover – Hulton Getty Collection. Cover mlb & b, 17m & 23t – Spectrum Colour Library. 5, 6-7t, 7tr & mr, 9ml & b, 13m, 14b, 17b, 18b, 19m & b, 20, 21t, 22t, 27m & 30 – Roger Vlitos. 8b, 19tr, 22m & b, 25m & 29m – Eye Ubiquitous. 12-13, 20-21, 23b, 28t & m – Science Photo Library. 14t – Bridgeman Art Library. 19tl & 25b – United States Department of Agriculture. 24m – James Davis Travel Photography.

32